mini *Paper Planes*

Small but Extraordinary Paper Planes You Can Make!

Michael Weinstein

Mud Puddle Books
NEW YORK

Mini Paper Planes:
Small but Extraordinary Paper Planes You Can Make!

Written by Michael Weinstein

Originally published in 2004 as
Stationery Flight:
Extraordinary Paper Planes

This edition published by
Mud Puddle Books, Inc.
54 W. 21st Street
Suite 601
New York, NY 10010
info@mudpuddlebooks.com

ISBN: 978-1-60311-050-1

Printed in China

Contents

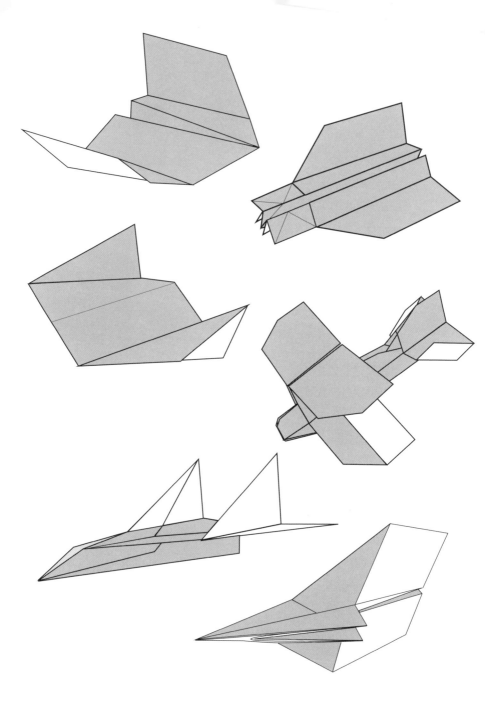

Why Paper Airplanes Fly:

Because we throw them.

This is partly correct. Any object will fly if given sufficient thrust. Rockets are simply engines with fins, and even your grandfather's Buick will fly if you attach a large enough engine (indeed its flight characteristics may even surpass its road handling). Paper airplanes are no different. Rocks fly just fine, as do dishes, crystal, and various other common household items. On the other hand, flying rocks and other items are not a very efficient use of energy. Hurled with the same force, a well-made paper airplane suited to high-speed launch will fly much farther than a rock. And it takes more fuel for a missile to traverse the same distance as an airplane. The reason is that airplanes, both paper and real, generate their own upward force, called lift. All objects in flight have a number of forces acting on them, including thrust, drag, weight, and lift:

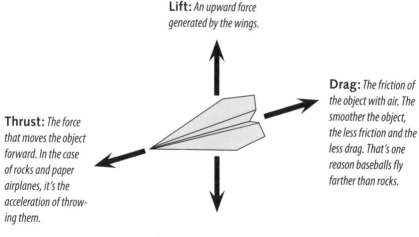

Lift: *An upward force generated by the wings.*

Drag: *The friction of the object with air. The smoother the object, the less friction and the less drag. That's one reason baseballs fly farther than rocks.*

Thrust: *The force that moves the object forward. In the case of rocks and paper airplanes, it's the acceleration of throwing them.*

Weight: *The Earth's gravity pulls any object toward the ground.*

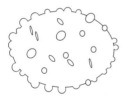

Rocks generate lift too, but very, very little. Baseballs actually generate lift in the direction of their spin, which is why a good pitcher can throw curve balls and sinkers.

So where does this lift stuff come from? Its existence comes from the fact that fluids (and gases, like air) exert less pressure when their velocity increases, as first described by an Italian named Bernoulli over two hundred years ago. To see how this affects airplanes, we need to examine an airplane's wing. The shape of a typical wing shows its curvature, or camber. The curve on the top of the wing, or airfoil, is what causes it to have lift. To see why, let's examine the travel of air across the wing.

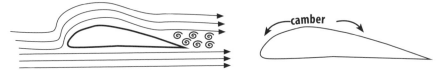

Notice that the air on the upper surface of the wing has to travel farther than the air on the bottom. Since it has to travel farther, the air on top speeds up. But remember Bernoulli? He discovered that when air speeds up, it exerts less pressure. Since the air on top exerts less pressure than the air on the bottom, there is a net upward force, or lift. All airplane wings exert lift, even paper ones. The little curlicues shown at the back of the wing represent turbulence, which is produced when air moves from regions of high to low velocity. This produces drag.

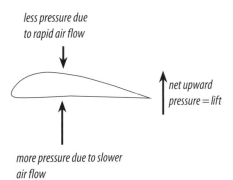

The more lift, the more drag. Airplanes have devices called flaps, which increase lift and drag, so that they can fly at lower speeds for landing. But now we run into a problem. Paper airplane wings are not curved, but are relatively flat. What gives?

To understand this, we have to talk about a long-deceased engineer named Osbourne Reynolds, who figured out how viscosity affects the behavior of liquids. Viscosity is an indication of the stickiness of a liquid or gas. Reynolds developed a formula to determine the effect of air on an object; thus every object has its own Reynolds number. For a paper airplane the number is in the tens of thousands, while it's in the millions for a real airplane. This means that from a paper airplane's perspective, air is very sticky. It is therefore hard for something tiny to produce lots of lift, but easy to make plenty of drag.

So paper airplanes have very thin wings, which produce less lift and less drag. Fortunately, paper is light, and little lift is needed to keep an average paper airplane aloft for the time it takes to traverse the living room. The effect of the Reynolds number can be seen in the shape of animal wings: bird wings are thick and shaped like an airfoil; bees have very flat wings, as they have lower Reynolds numbers and are governed by the viscosity of air. Real airplanes are so large that the camber of their wings is easily visible.

The length of the wing is referred to as its **chord**, while the distance across is its **span**. Wingspan divided by wing chord equals the **aspect ratio**, an important measure of how much drag a wing will produce. Swept-back wings have a low aspect ratio, and produce little drag. Rectangular, thick wings produce more. We can see how the shape of the wing affects the flight of a paper airplane with a couple of examples.

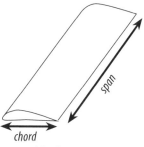

chord

span / chord = Aspect Ratio

Example 1:

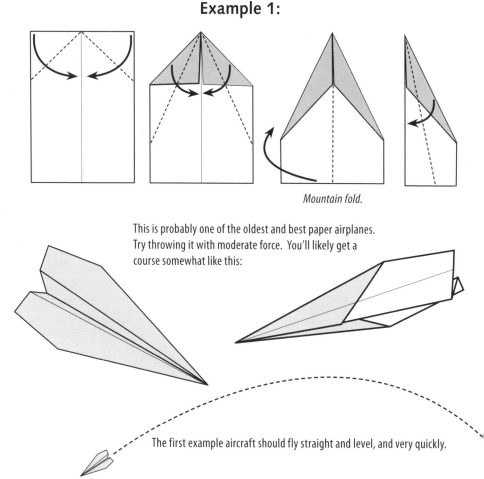

Mountain fold.

This is probably one of the oldest and best paper airplanes. Try throwing it with moderate force. You'll likely get a course somewhat like this:

The first example aircraft should fly straight and level, and very quickly.

Example 2:

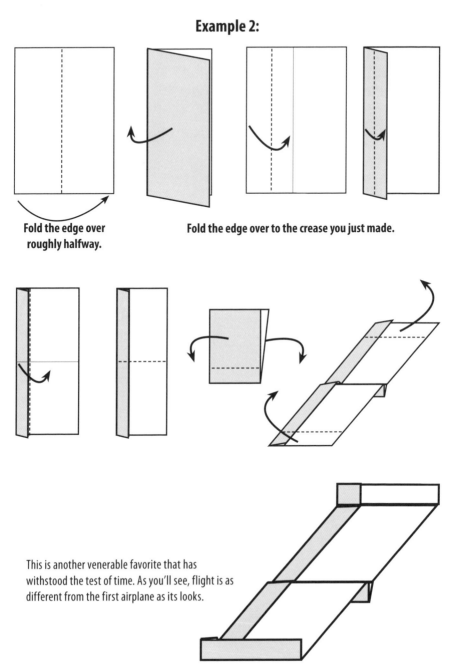

Fold the edge over roughly halfway.

Fold the edge over to the crease you just made.

This is another venerable favorite that has withstood the test of time. As you'll see, flight is as different from the first airplane as its looks.

Try throwing this airplane as you did the first. See the difference? This airplane shoots up instead of flying straight and level. Since lift depends on thrust, you can try giving it a lighter throw to get less of an upward course. You'll notice that the airplane flies more slowly than the first. Why? There are some obvious differences between these two airplanes. For instance, one has swept-back wings, while the other has straight wings. How does that affect the aspect ratio?

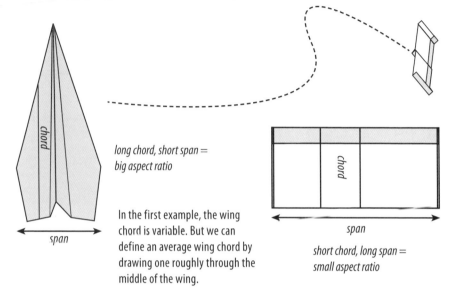

long chord, short span =
big aspect ratio

In the first example, the wing chord is variable. But we can define an average wing chord by drawing one roughly through the middle of the wing.

short chord, long span =
small aspect ratio

Notice that the faster airplane has a longer chord and smaller span, which makes its aspect ratio much higher, and reduces drag. That's one reason why Example 2 flies so much more slowly. But Example 2 also shows much more lift than Example 1. Why ? To answer that question we should look at a cross-section of the two wings:

Example 1

Example 2

The wing in Example 2 resembles an airfoil much more closely than Example 1. It therefore produces more lift and tends to nose up. It also produces more drag, so it slows down. This combination of factors affects many of the paper airplanes you will be folding, and can be used to get better, or more customized flight from an airplane. But there are other good ways to make the same airplane fly very different flight paths. A normal airplane has to ascend, descend, turn, and do many other things. Both paper and real airplanes use **trim** to fly the way their pilots want.

Trim

You can further control the flight of your airplane by using control surfaces and trim. Real airplanes have a number of these control surfaces, including elevators, ailerons, and rudder. The elevators control the pitch, or whether the airplane points up or down. That can be handy if you want to take off or land. The rudder turns the aircraft left or right, and is said (in pilot lingo) to control the yaw. The ailerons control whether the wings are level, or are canted at an angle. This is called **roll**, and the angle between the wings and the ground is called the **angle of bank**.

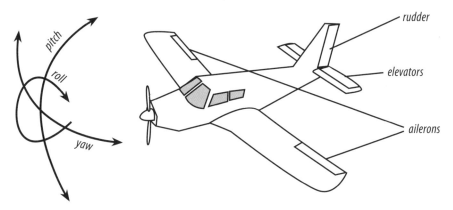

Paper airplanes also have control surfaces. This can be demonstrated by giving Example Airplane 1 elevators. Fold Example Airplane 1 and throw it. Notice how it flies. Now, fold small flaps up in the rear of the wings. These will act like the elevators in a real airplane. Notice how this affects the plane's performance.

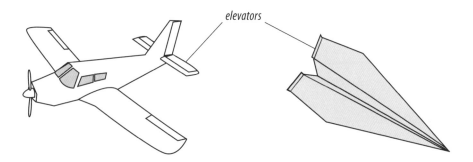

The elevator tends to force the tail end of the aircraft down and the nose up, causing it to fly a higher course. Of course, the elevators also increase drag, causing the plane to fly more slowly.

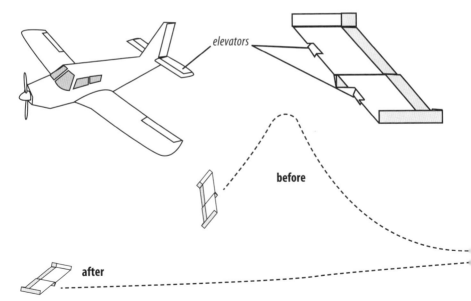

On a real airplane, the elevator can also be used to point the nose down for descent. You can do the same thing with a paper plane. Example Airplane 1 is not in need of any down elevator, but Example Airplane 2 could use some to straighten out its course. Fold Example Airplane 2, and give it some down elevator by making small flaps in the back and bending them down. This should bring the rear of the airplane up and the nose down, leveling off an otherwise unstable flight. Elevator can be used to give an airplane a smoother course, or to give its flight an upward or downward path, depending on what you like. The important thing is that it gives you a chance to decide how your airplane will fly.

elevators

before

after

You can do more with trim than just level out an airplane's flight. Using horizontal and vertical control surfaces, you can make your airplane do almost anything you want.

11

The flaps on paper airplanes can also be used as ailerons, which bank real airplanes in order to turn them. Bicycles, motorcycles, and speedboats also bank in turns. To give your airplane ailerons, bend one flap up and the other down.

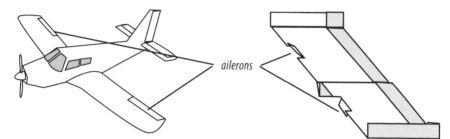

ailerons

Try giving this airplane a really gentle throw, and watch carefully. You'll see the wings start going at an angle, and the entire plane should turn to one side.

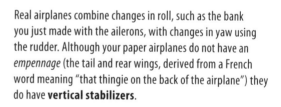

Real airplanes combine changes in roll, such as the bank you just made with the ailerons, with changes in yaw using the rudder. Although your paper airplanes do not have an *empennage* (the tail and rear wings, derived from a French word meaning "that thingie on the back of the airplane") they do have **vertical stabilizers**.

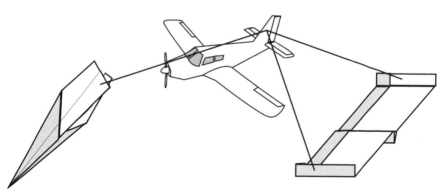

You can use the vertical stabilizers of your example airplanes for rudders to make them turn in flight. Try bending the vertical stabilizers of Example Airplane 2. It's a bit tricky, as the vertical stabilizers are attached to the wing, but it can be done. Now give the plane an easy toss. Notice how it adopts a turning flight, similar to what it did with the aileron adjustments? Now "for the cat's meow", combine the ailerons with the rudder. You can use these adjustments to get a number of different flight characteristics out of the same airplane! Example Airplane 2 is not the best airplane on which to use trim, as the vertical control surfaces are small, and the aspect ratio is extreme. Example Airplane 1 suffers similarly. But, there are lots of planes in *Mini Paper Planes* that have nice big control surfaces and intermediate aspect ratios, you can try all different kinds of trim!

Dihedral

The next time you're at your local airport, have a look at the airplanes, and look closely at the wings. You'll find that they're slightly upswept, like the Piper Cherokee shown. This wing angle, called *dihedral*, can stabilize an aircraft along its longitudinal axis, from front to back.

Normal airplanes have a limit to the amount of dihedral they can use, because if they have too much they go into what's known as a Dutch Roll, which involves really scary back-and-forth movements of the plane. The good thing is that paper airplanes don't Dutch Roll (or if they do it isn't scary, since you're on the ground), so you can use just as much dihedral as you like to stabilize an airplane in flight. Notice that dihedral is an upward angle.

Downward angle, or *anhedral*, is used in some really swoopy fighter jets, but it usually doesn't work very well in paper airplanes. Each airplane has a front view where the recommended dihedral and angles for vertical stabilizers are shown. However, every airplane is a bit different, so feel free to play with the trim and dihedral to make the plane do what you want.

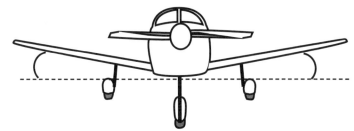

dihedral angle

Symbols

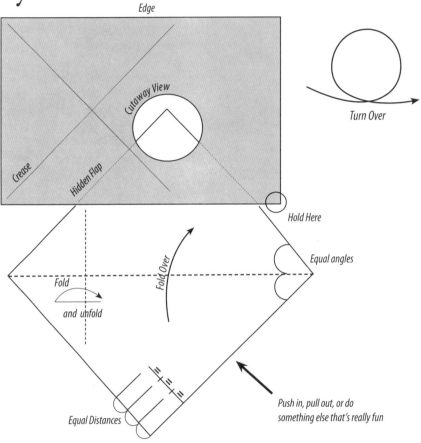

Edge

Cutaway View

Crease

Hidden Flap

Turn Over

Hold Here

Equal angles

Fold
and unfold

Fold Over

Equal Distances

Push in, pull out, or do
something else that's really fun

Valley fold
Fold so the crease points away from you (and the flap toward you).

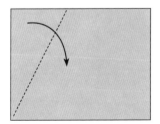

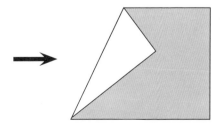

Mountain fold
Fold so that the crease points toward you (and the flap away from you).

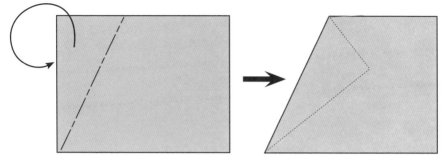

Inside Reverse fold
Fold so that a point falls between layers.

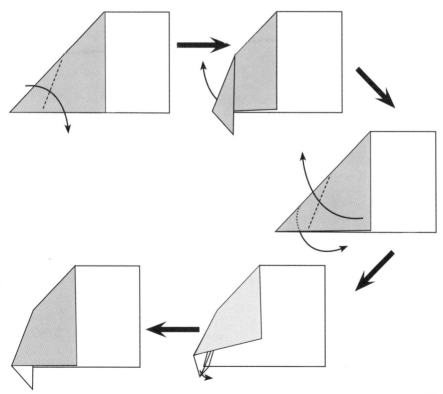

Outside Reverse fold
Fold so that a point wraps around the outside of two layers.

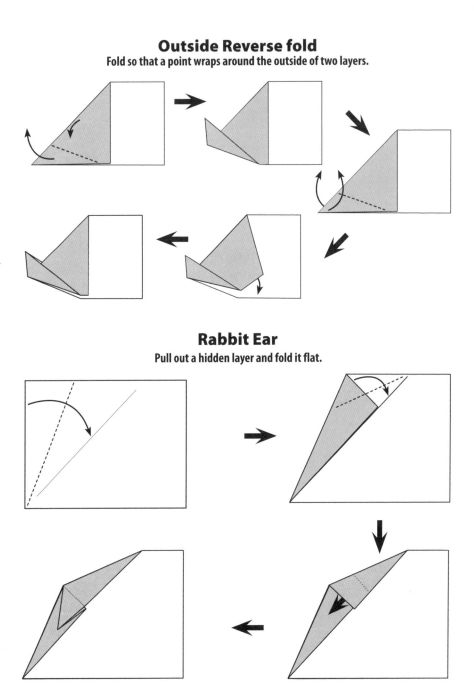

Rabbit Ear
Pull out a hidden layer and fold it flat.

Squash fold

Separate two adjacent layers and flatten the pocket that forms between them.

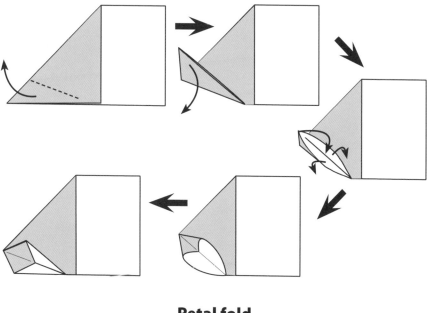

Petal fold

Separate two layers while flattening the pockets that form on either side.

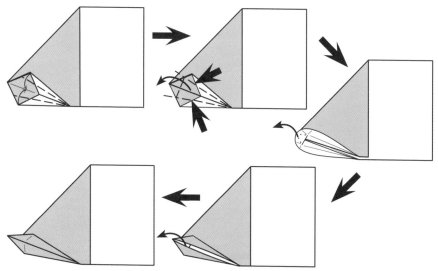

Sink fold

A multi-layered point gets pushed to the inside. The point is partially unfolded and mountain folded at the desired position.

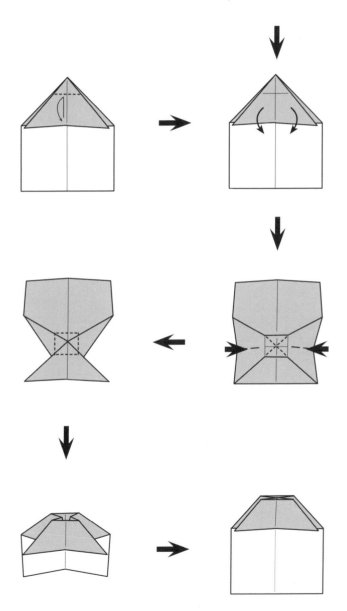

Paper Airplane Bases

Origami models often involve the same steps at the beginning. For example, if you wanted to fold a bird, you would need a head, neck, tail, and wings. In fact, one of the classic origami bases is the bird base, from which these structures are easily derived. The origami genius John Montrol has developed a dog base, from which one can readily fold the parts needed for a four-footed animal. Many of the airplanes in this book are derived from a set of common precursors, instructions for which follow on the next page. The Airplane Base is short, and generates two evenly sized sets of wings. The Canard Base is the basis for most of the canard, or forward-wing aircraft.

Airplane Base

This will make two sets of wings, or one set of wings and one set of...

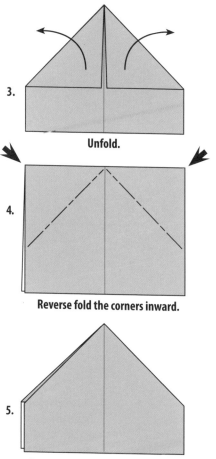

1.

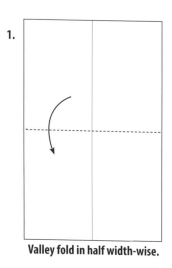

Valley fold in half width-wise.

2.

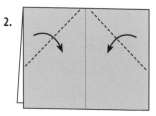

Valley fold both corners to the center.

3.

Unfold.

4.

Reverse fold the corners inward.

5.

Paper airplane base #1 complete.

Canard Base

This base makes it easy to design canard, or forward-wing aircraft, because it generates two flaps in the front that can easily be manipulated to make many shapes and do a number of interesting things.

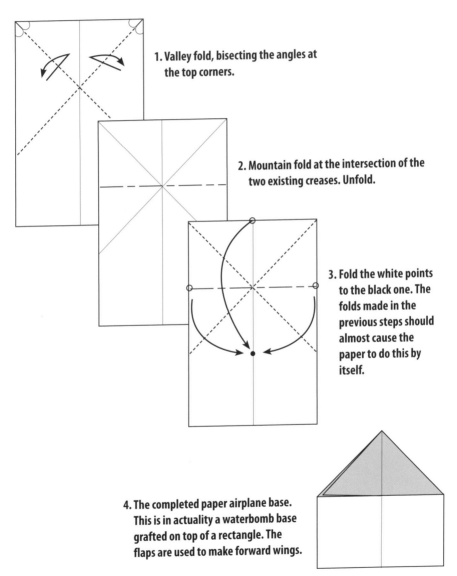

1. Valley fold, bisecting the angles at the top corners.

2. Mountain fold at the intersection of the two existing creases. Unfold.

3. Fold the white points to the black one. The folds made in the previous steps should almost cause the paper to do this by itself.

4. The completed paper airplane base. This is in actuality a waterbomb base grafted on top of a rectangle. The flaps are used to make forward wings.

Making and flying paper airplanes is educational, recreational, environmental (all that recycling of paper) and just plain fun. There are, of course, a few things that aid in the pursuit of the perfect plane.

Paper

Many kinds of paper are good for the aspiring parchment pilot. All of them are reasonably thick and strong; newspaper makes lousy fighter bombers, for instance. On the other hand, too much thickness spoils the party. Posterboard makes for really tough Origami, and most reasonably cool paper airplanes wouldn't dream of being made from construction paper. The paper must also hold a crease fairly well, so most softer papers are way out of it. Copier paper is one of my favorites, as it combines strength, light weight, and durability.

Amost all of the airplanes here are made from paper that is 8½ × 5½ inches (A5-size). This is not some mysterious paper only available in the finer bookstores of Tibet, but is a half sheet of ordinary 8½ × 11 inch (A-4 size) paper, available everywhere. When creating my cellulose squadron I noticed that a normal-sized piece of paper was sort of short and didn't leave me much room to play around and do fun and interesting things (like use a Pagoda to create Canard wings). I found that a half-sheet was longer, and more fun to create with.

The craft contained within are all indoor flyers (growing up in northern Ohio, we had to appreciate good-weather days, all two of them). Being manufactured from smaller paper makes them lighter and more nimble than their larger brethren. Making the required size of paper is very simple; fold an 8½ × 11 (A4-size) piece of paper in half, and cut along the crease. A paper-cutter makes it even easier. If you're locked in a room with none of these things, you can simply tear a piece of paper in half.

How to Make an 8½ × 5½ Inch (A5-size) Sheet of Paper

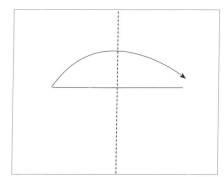

Fold an 8½ × 11 inch (A4-size) sheet of paper in half, and crease really well. Unfold.

Hold the paper so the crease faces up toward you. Pull evenly around the crease at the part nearest to you.

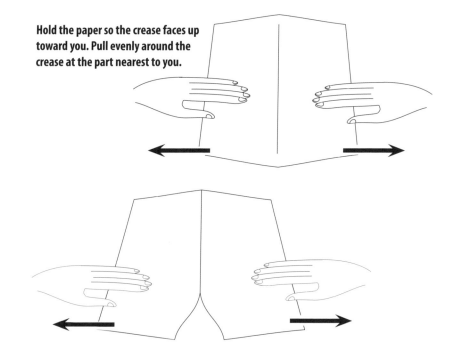

The paper should start to tear where the midline crease meets the forward edge. Continue to apply pressure evenly, and the paper will tear very neatly in half. With a bit of practice, this becomes really easy, and faster than scissors!

The Planes

Have fun and happy landings!

Thirdsies

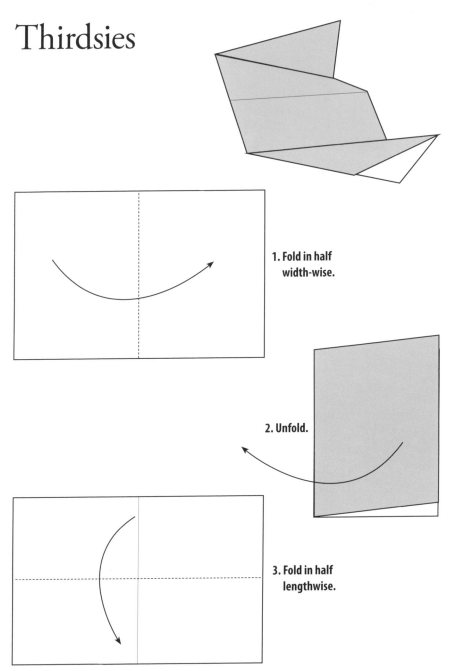

1. Fold in half width-wise.

2. Unfold.

3. Fold in half lengthwise.

4. Unfold.

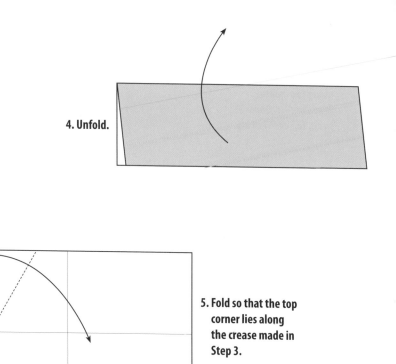

5. Fold so that the top corner lies along the crease made in Step 3.

6. Like so. Unfold, and repeat on the other side.

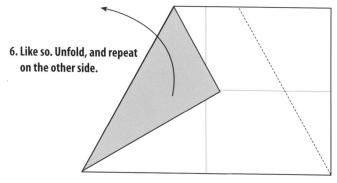

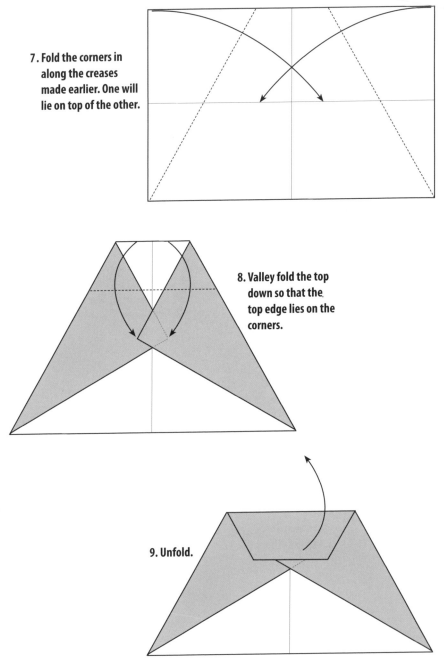

7. Fold the corners in along the creases made earlier. One will lie on top of the other.

8. Valley fold the top down so that the top edge lies on the corners.

9. Unfold.

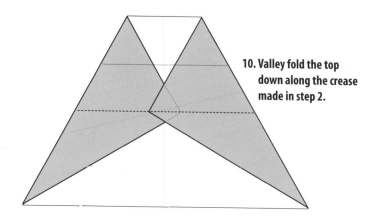

10. Valley fold the top down along the crease made in step 2.

11. Mountain fold the top all the way underneath.

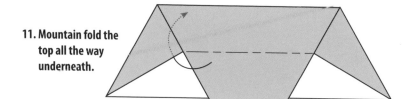

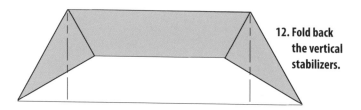

12. Fold back the vertical stabilizers.

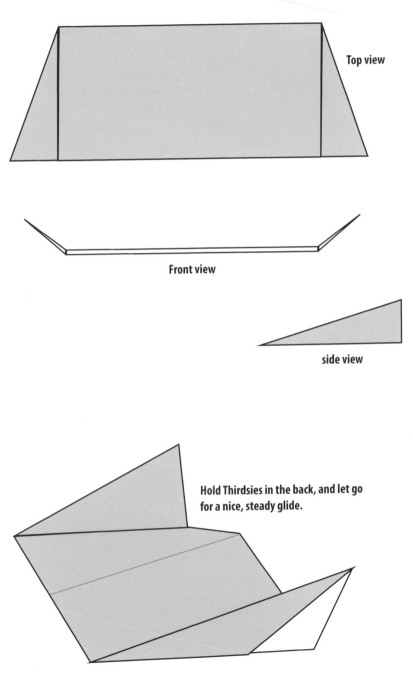

Top view

Front view

side view

Hold Thirdsies in the back, and let go
for a nice, steady glide.

Bottlenose

Start with an 8½ × 5½ inch (A5-size) sheet of paper creased in half lengthwise.

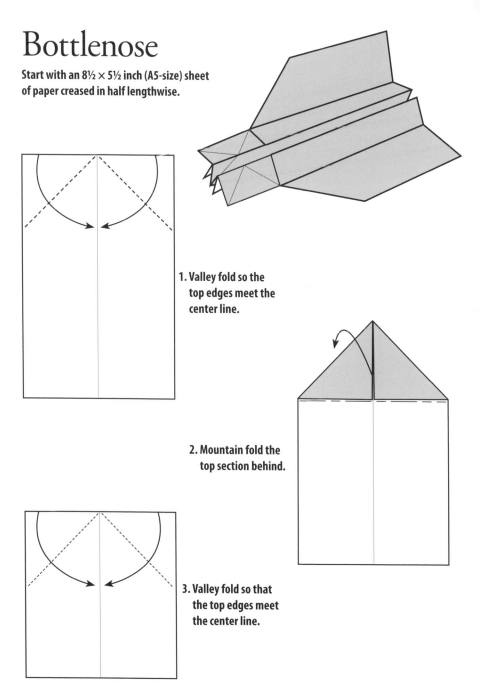

1. Valley fold so the top edges meet the center line.

2. Mountain fold the top section behind.

3. Valley fold so that the top edges meet the center line.

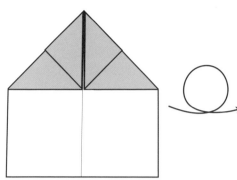

4. Turn over.

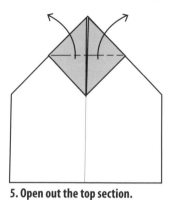

5. Open out the top section.

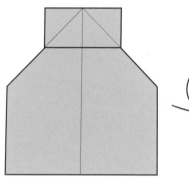

6. Turn over.

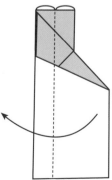

7. Mountain fold the flaps underneath to thicken the leading edges of the wing and move weight forward.

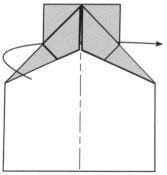

8. Mountain fold the model in half lengthwise.

9. Valley fold the wings down by folding halfway across the top.

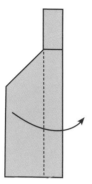

10. Valley fold a vertical stabilizer.

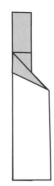

11. The completed Bottlenose.

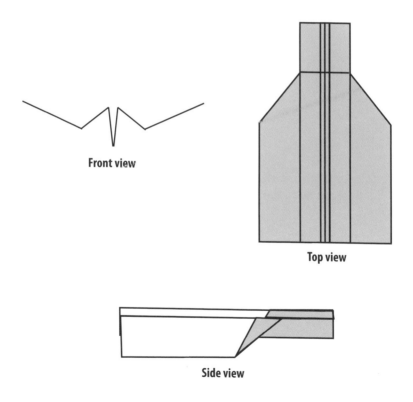

Front view

Top view

Side view

Raptor

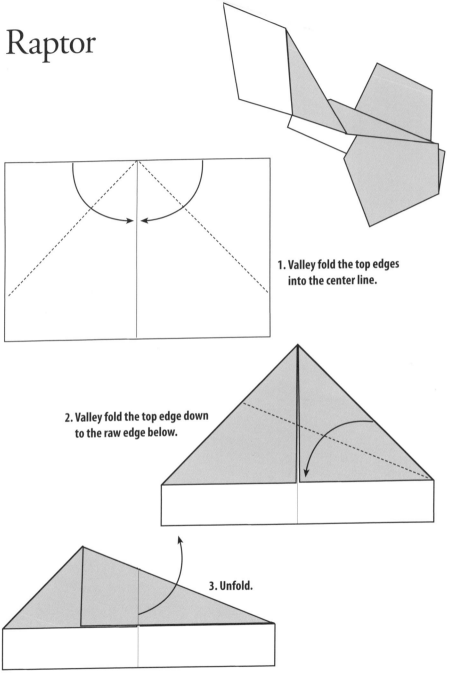

1. Valley fold the top edges into the center line.

2. Valley fold the top edge down to the raw edge below.

3. Unfold.

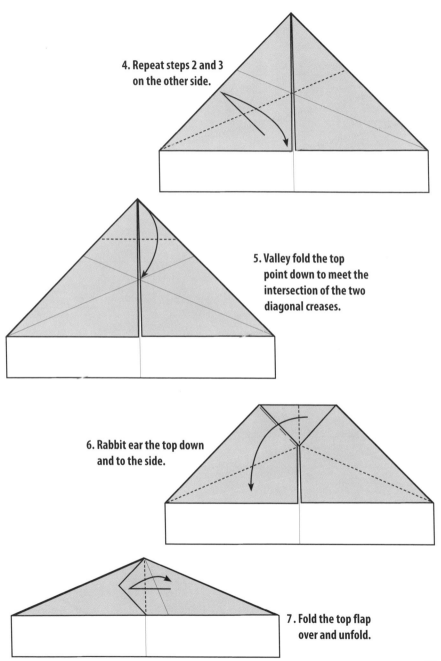

4. Repeat steps 2 and 3 on the other side.

5. Valley fold the top point down to meet the intersection of the two diagonal creases.

6. Rabbit ear the top down and to the side.

7. Fold the top flap over and unfold.

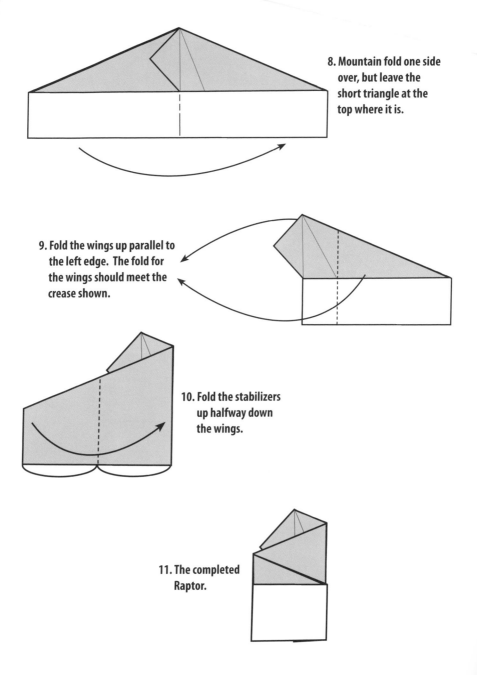

8. Mountain fold one side over, but leave the short triangle at the top where it is.

9. Fold the wings up parallel to the left edge. The fold for the wings should meet the crease shown.

10. Fold the stabilizers up halfway down the wings.

11. The completed Raptor.

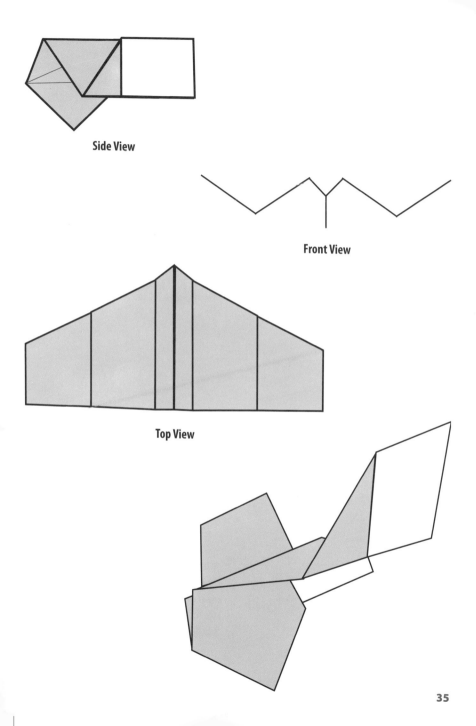

Side View

Front View

Top View

Skeeter

Thrown hard or soft, Skeeter will give a good flight every time. The folding gets a little bit more complicated, though.

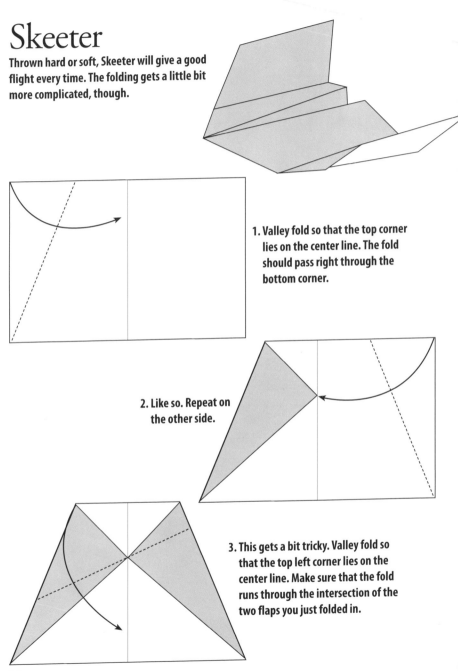

1. Valley fold so that the top corner lies on the center line. The fold should pass right through the bottom corner.

2. Like so. Repeat on the other side.

3. This gets a bit tricky. Valley fold so that the top left corner lies on the center line. Make sure that the fold runs through the intersection of the two flaps you just folded in.

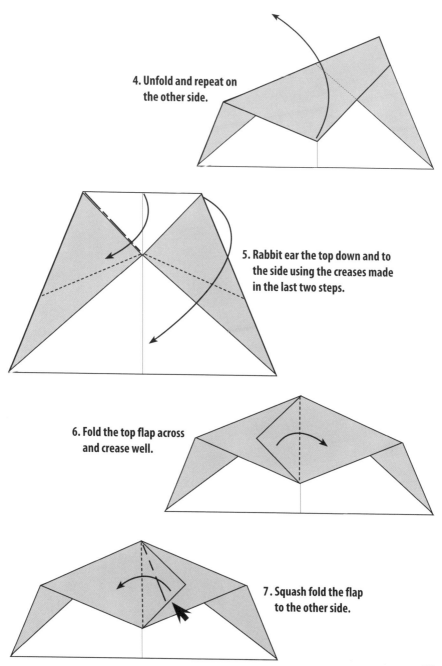

4. Unfold and repeat on the other side.

5. Rabbit ear the top down and to the side using the creases made in the last two steps.

6. Fold the top flap across and crease well.

7. Squash fold the flap to the other side.

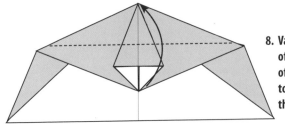

8. Valley fold the bottom point of the top layer (it consists of paired white flaps) to the topmost point. Carefully fold through all the layers.

9. Unfold.

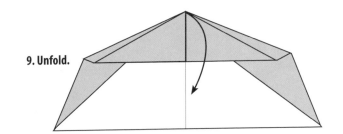

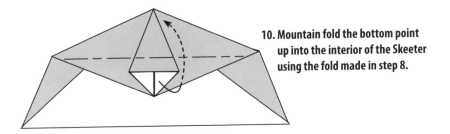

10. Mountain fold the bottom point up into the interior of the Skeeter using the fold made in step 8.

11. Mountain fold in half.

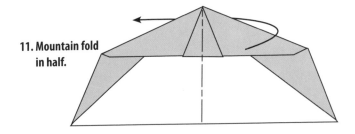

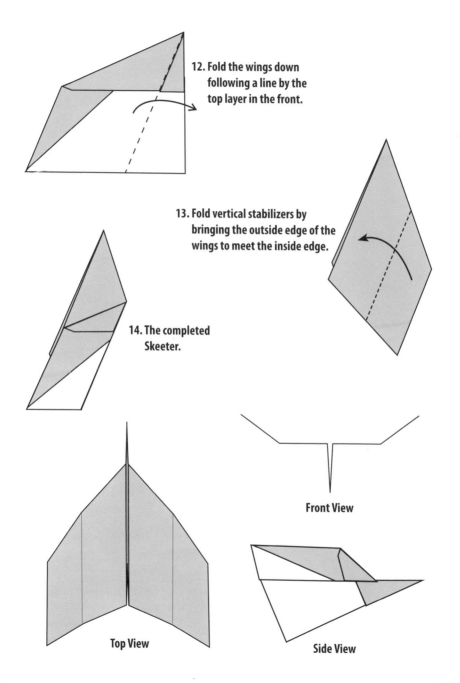

12. Fold the wings down following a line by the top layer in the front.

13. Fold vertical stabilizers by bringing the outside edge of the wings to meet the inside edge.

14. The completed Skeeter.

Front View

Top View

Side View

Glider Supreme

Start with an 8½ × 5½ inch (A5-size) sheet of paper creased in half lengthwise. The paper should always be creased in the middle to preserve symmetry.

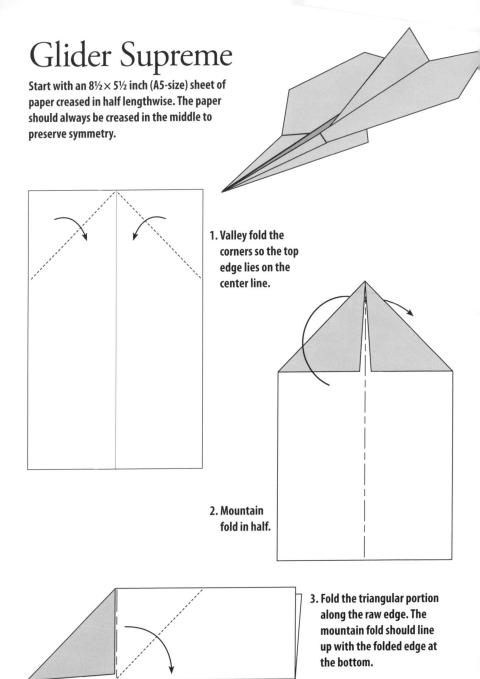

1. Valley fold the corners so the top edge lies on the center line.

2. Mountain fold in half.

3. Fold the triangular portion along the raw edge. The mountain fold should line up with the folded edge at the bottom.

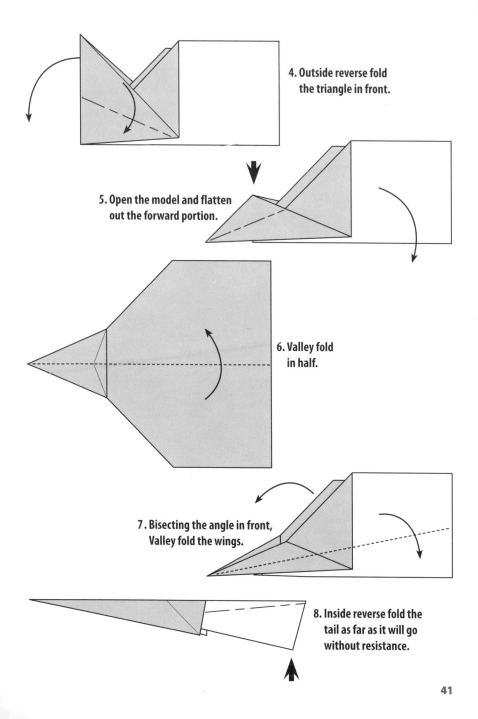

4. Outside reverse fold the triangle in front.

5. Open the model and flatten out the forward portion.

6. Valley fold in half.

7. Bisecting the angle in front, Valley fold the wings.

8. Inside reverse fold the tail as far as it will go without resistance.

41

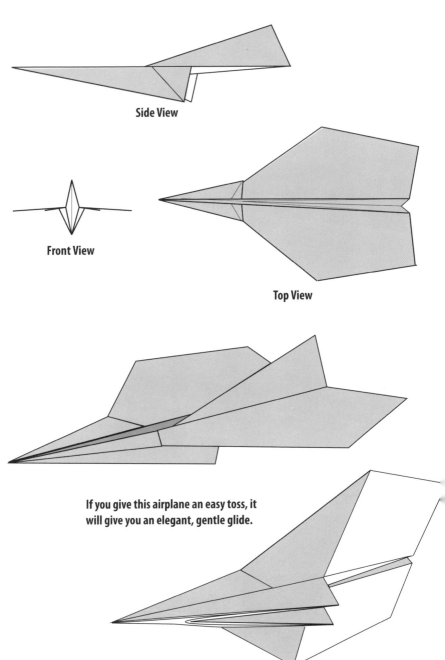

Side View

Front View

Top View

If you give this airplane an easy toss, it
will give you an elegant, gentle glide.

Elapse

Elapse presents large control surfaces, and can be trimmed to do a great many things. Start with a sheet of paper creased in half lengthwise.

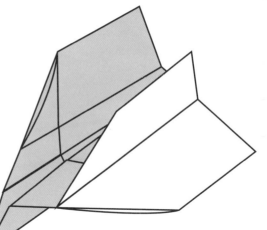

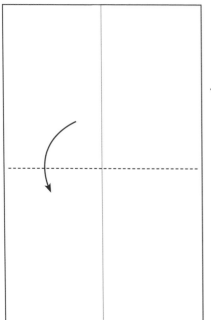

1. Valley fold in half widthwise.

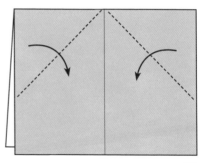

2. Valley fold both corners to the center.

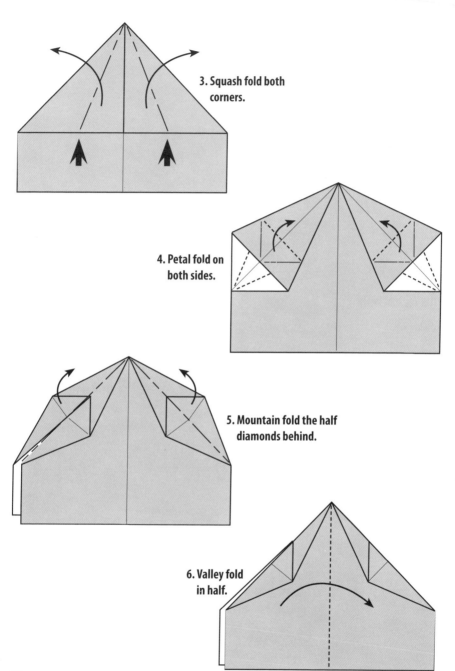

3. Squash fold both corners.

4. Petal fold on both sides.

5. Mountain fold the half diamonds behind.

6. Valley fold in half.

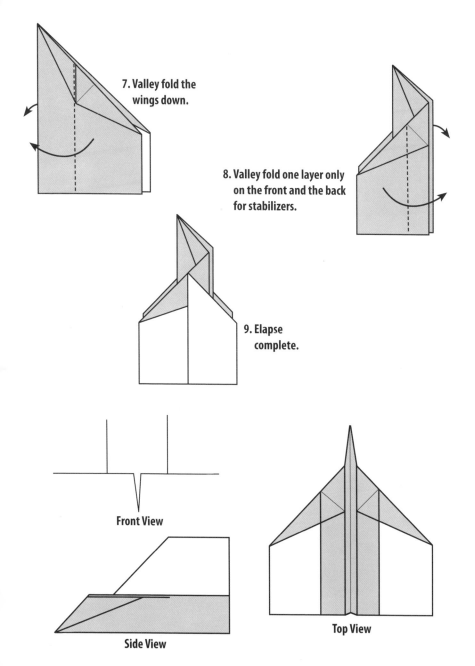

7. Valley fold the wings down.

8. Valley fold one layer only on the front and the back for stabilizers.

9. Elapse complete.

Front View

Side View

Top View

F-14

This sleek design reminds me of an F-14 Tomcat in supersonic flight. Start with a sheet of paper folded in half and creased down the middle.

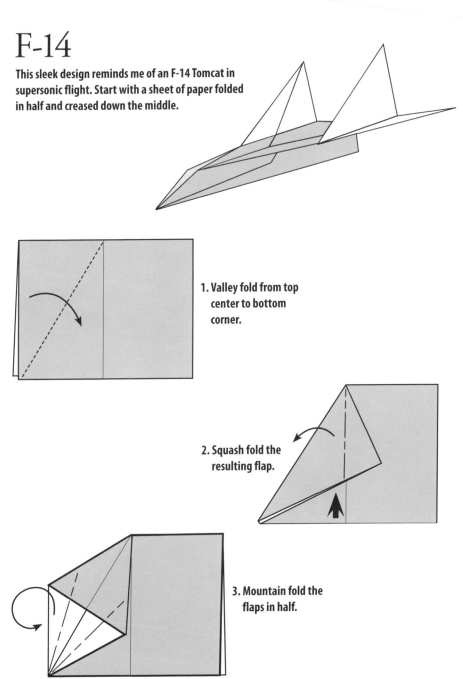

1. Valley fold from top center to bottom corner.

2. Squash fold the resulting flap.

3. Mountain fold the flaps in half.

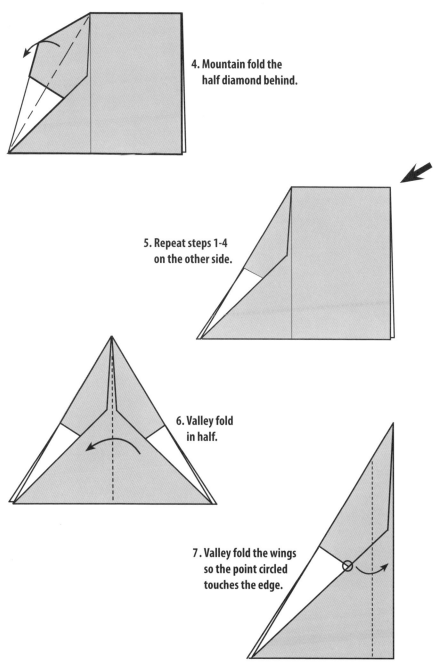

4. Mountain fold the half diamond behind.

5. Repeat steps 1-4 on the other side.

6. Valley fold in half.

7. Valley fold the wings so the point circled touches the edge.

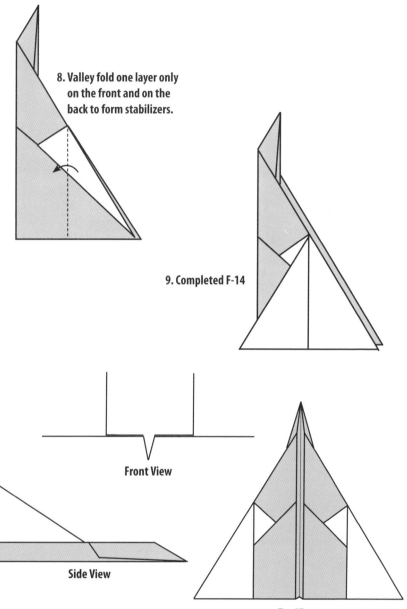

8. Valley fold one layer only on the front and on the back to form stabilizers.

9. Completed F-14

Front View

Side View

Top View

Omega Flyer

Another good stunt airplane; begin with the Airplane Base.

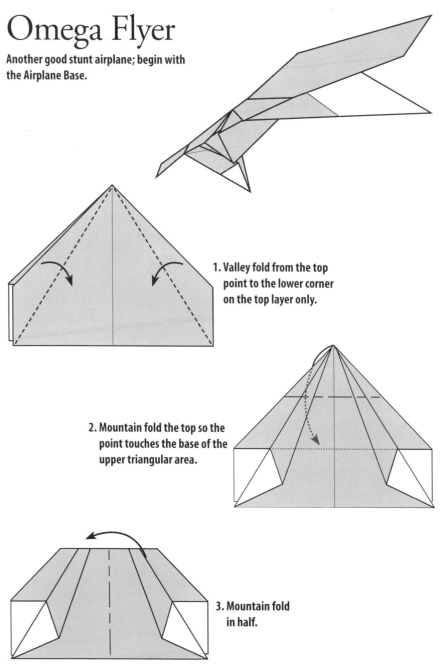

1. Valley fold from the top point to the lower corner on the top layer only.

2. Mountain fold the top so the point touches the base of the upper triangular area.

3. Mountain fold in half.

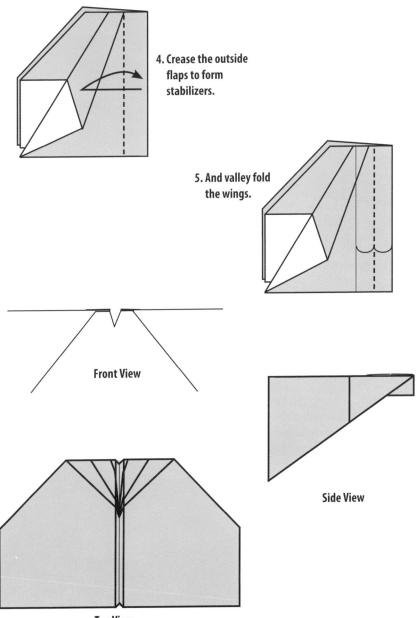

4. Crease the outside flaps to form stabilizers.

5. And valley fold the wings.

Front View

Side View

Top View

Loopmaker

An excellent plane that can be adjusted to do all manner of
stunts, including loops. Begin with the Canard Base.

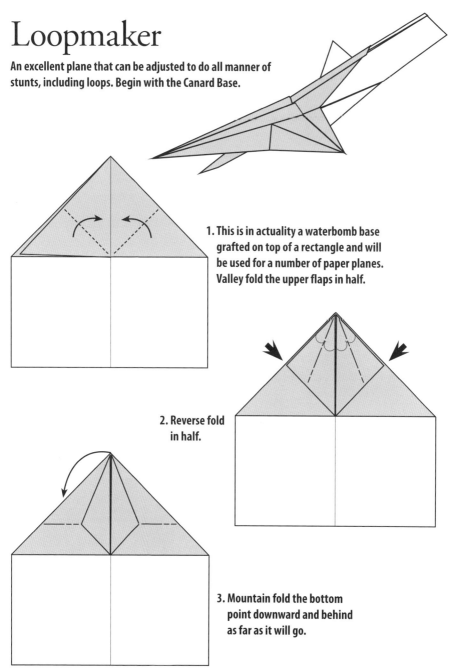

1. This is in actuality a waterbomb base
   grafted on top of a rectangle and will
   be used for a number of paper planes.
   Valley fold the upper flaps in half.

2. Reverse fold
   in half.

3. Mountain fold the bottom
   point downward and behind
   as far as it will go.

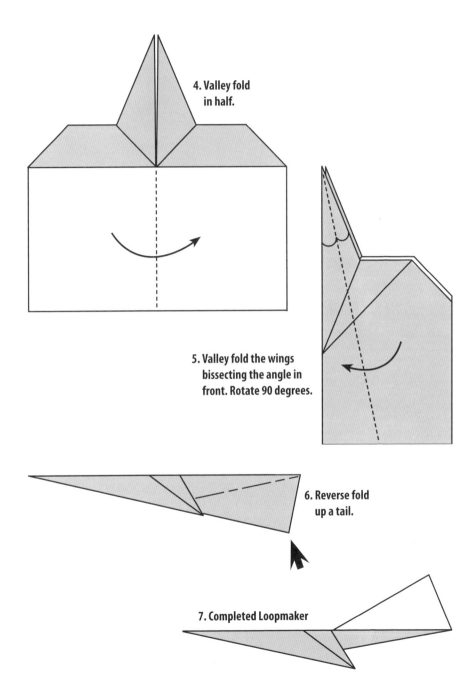

4. Valley fold in half.

5. Valley fold the wings bissecting the angle in front. Rotate 90 degrees.

6. Reverse fold up a tail.

7. Completed Loopmaker

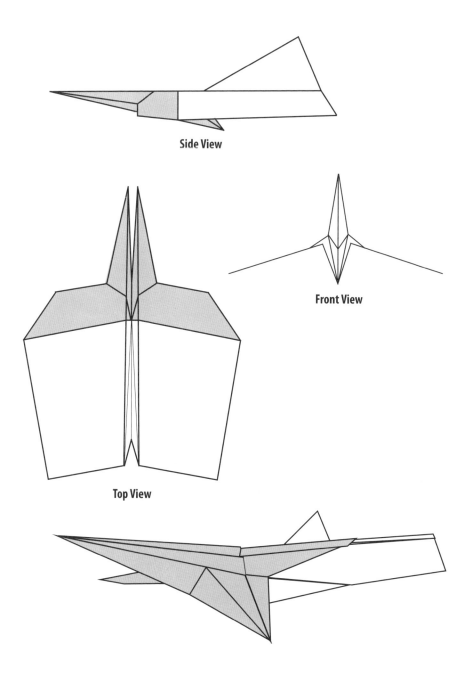

Side View

Front View

Top View

Mach II

This is one of my best flyers.
Start with the Airplane Base.

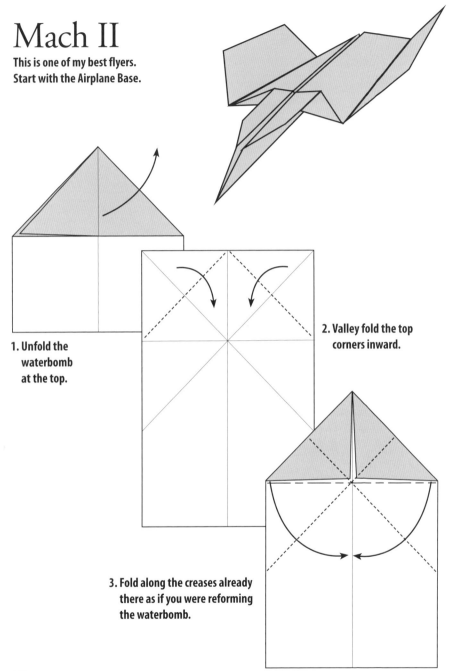

1. Unfold the waterbomb at the top.

2. Valley fold the top corners inward.

3. Fold along the creases already there as if you were reforming the waterbomb.

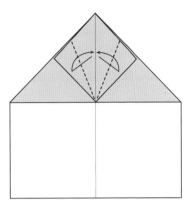

4. Fold the triangular flaps so their lower edges lie along the center line. Crease well, then unfold.

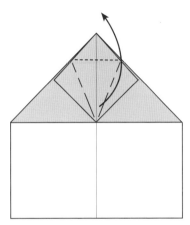

5. Petal fold the top layer upward.

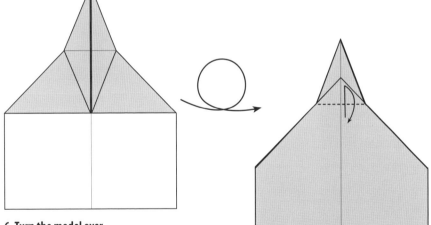

6. Turn the model over.

7. Valley fold the shorter of the two triangles at the top at its base. Crease well and unfold.

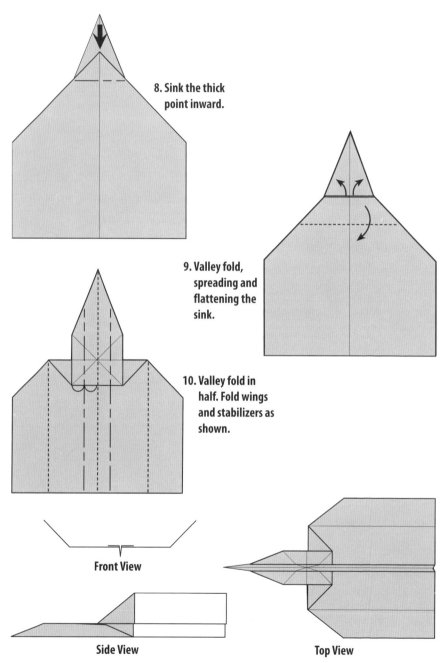

8. Sink the thick point inward.

9. Valley fold, spreading and flattening the sink.

10. Valley fold in half. Fold wings and stabilizers as shown.

Front View

Side View

Top View

56

Multi-Stage Craft

Start with an 8½× 5½ inch (A5-size) sheet of paper creased down the middle.

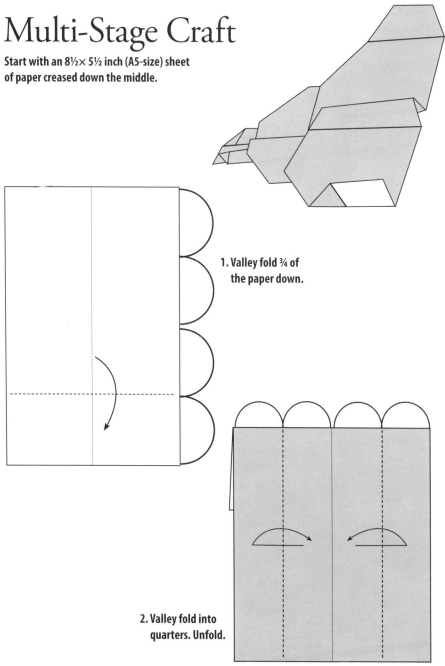

1. Valley fold ¾ of the paper down.

2. Valley fold into quarters. Unfold.

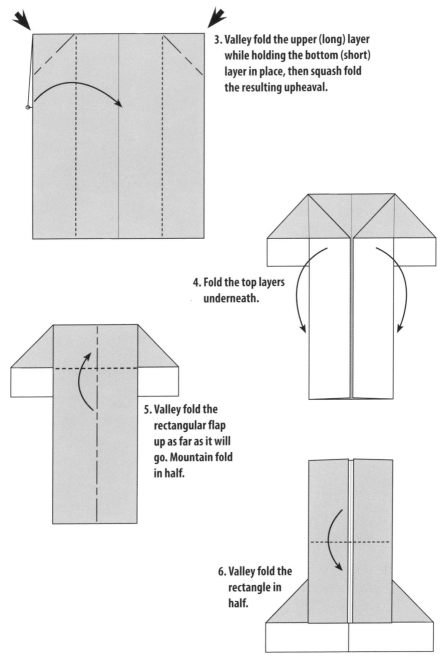

3. Valley fold the upper (long) layer while holding the bottom (short) layer in place, then squash fold the resulting upheaval.

4. Fold the top layers underneath.

5. Valley fold the rectangular flap up as far as it will go. Mountain fold in half.

6. Valley fold the rectangle in half.

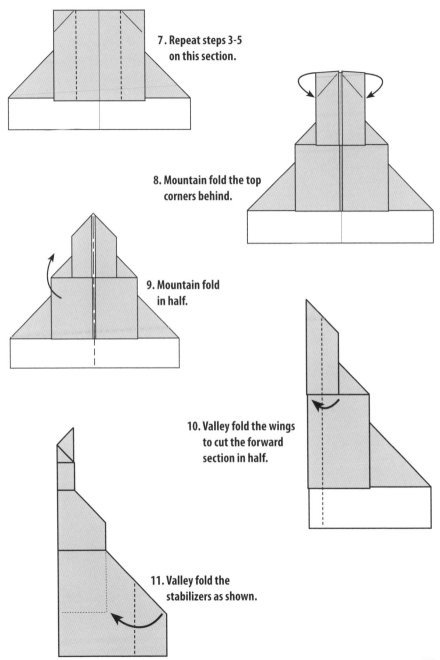

7. Repeat steps 3-5 on this section.

8. Mountain fold the top corners behind.

9. Mountain fold in half.

10. Valley fold the wings to cut the forward section in half.

11. Valley fold the stabilizers as shown.

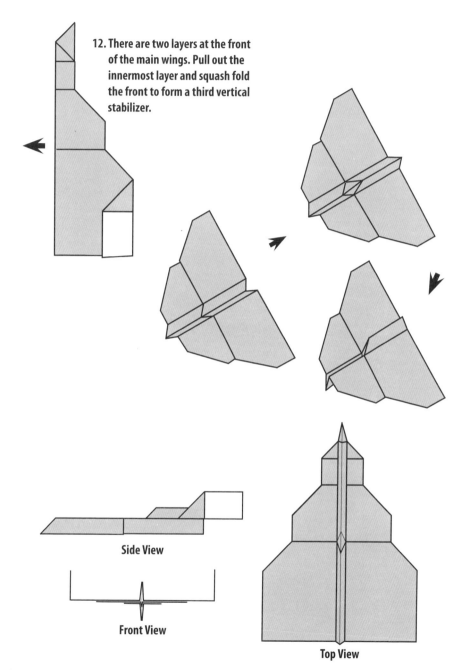

12. There are two layers at the front of the main wings. Pull out the innermost layer and squash fold the front to form a third vertical stabilizer.

Side View

Front View

Top View

Aerobotch

This ungainly little plane makes a superb dart. Its large control surfaces can also be used to create many maneuvers and stunts. Start with the Airplane Base.

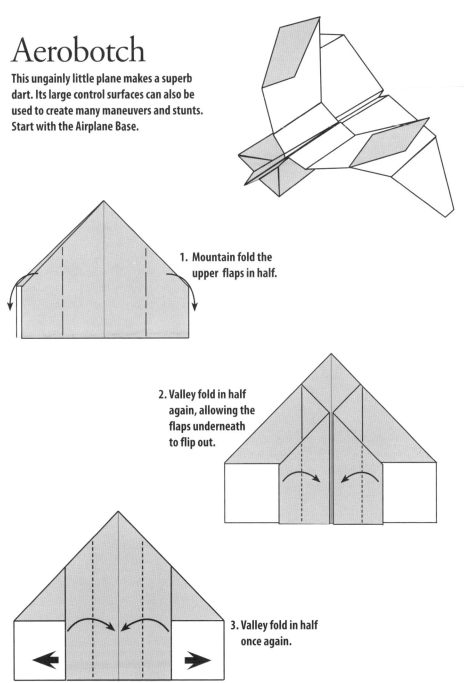

1. Mountain fold the upper flaps in half.

2. Valley fold in half again, allowing the flaps underneath to flip out.

3. Valley fold in half once again.

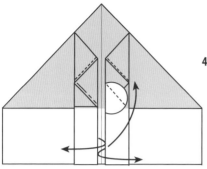

4. Now for the fun part: Squash fold the top layer upward following the upper diagonal folds. At the same time you'll have to squash fold a pocket that forms underneath.

5. Squash fold the upper flap downward.

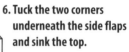

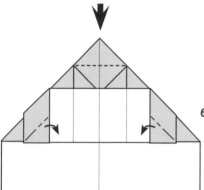

6. Tuck the two corners underneath the side flaps and sink the top.

7. Turn the model over.

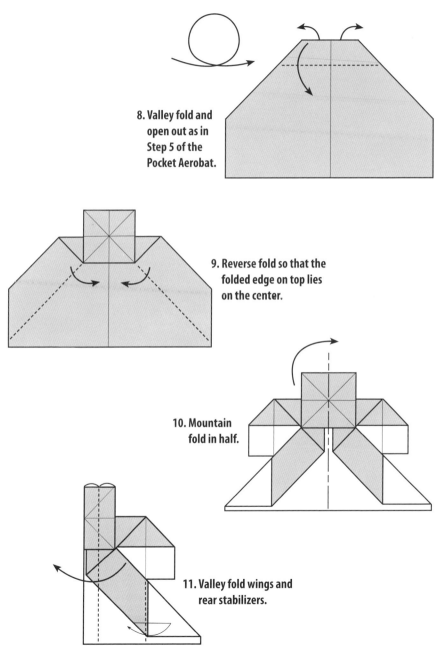

8. Valley fold and open out as in Step 5 of the Pocket Aerobat.

9. Reverse fold so that the folded edge on top lies on the center.

10. Mountain fold in half.

11. Valley fold wings and rear stabilizers.

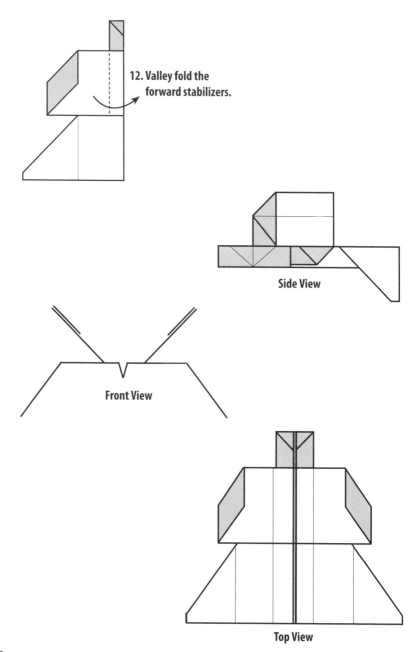

12. Valley fold the forward stabilizers.

Side View

Front View

Top View

Hammerhead

For this canard begin with Step 2 of the Loopmaker.

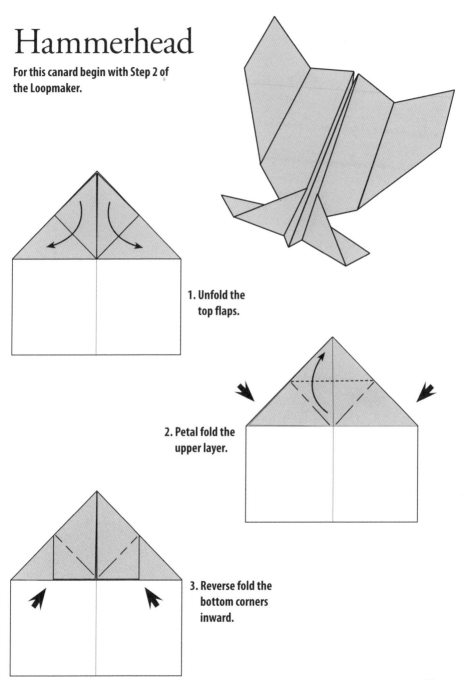

1. Unfold the top flaps.

2. Petal fold the upper layer.

3. Reverse fold the bottom corners inward.

4. Bisecting the angles at the top, squash fold the upper flaps to the outside.

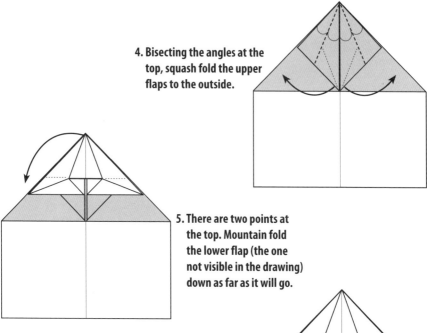

5. There are two points at the top. Mountain fold the lower flap (the one not visible in the drawing) down as far as it will go.

6. Valley fold to form the forward edges of the wings so that the top edge of the wing section (which lies between two layers and is not visible in the diagram) touches the center line.

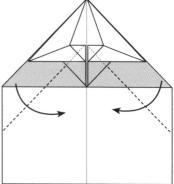

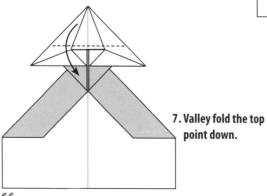

7. Valley fold the top point down.

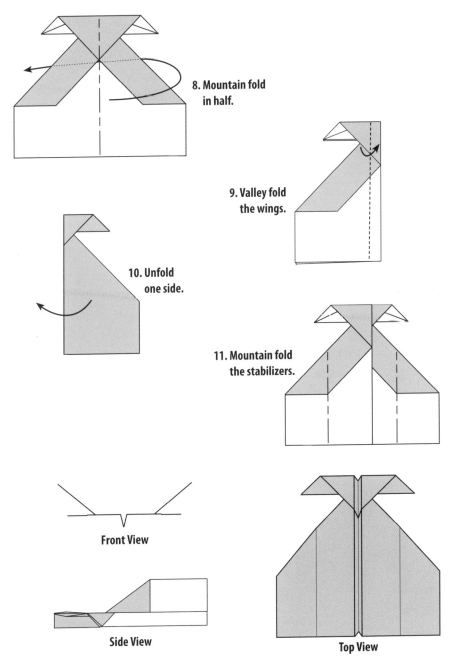

8. Mountain fold in half.

9. Valley fold the wings.

10. Unfold one side.

11. Mountain fold the stabilizers.

Front View

Side View

Top View

Pagodor Volant

A long time ago I tried mounting a traditional Chinese pagoda on the end of a rectangle to make an airplane. What I got was this interesting delta-winged canard with a trick front end. Begin (once again) with Loopmaker, Step 2.

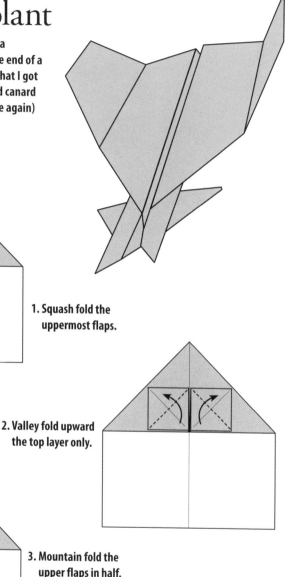

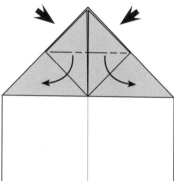

1. Squash fold the uppermost flaps.

2. Valley fold upward the top layer only.

3. Mountain fold the upper flaps in half.

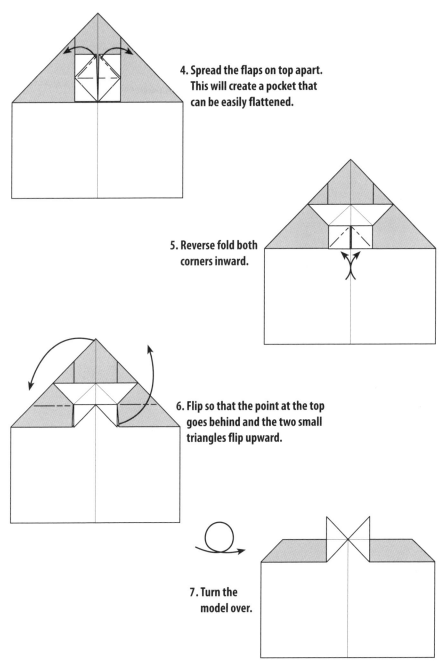

4. Spread the flaps on top apart. This will create a pocket that can be easily flattened.

5. Reverse fold both corners inward.

6. Flip so that the point at the top goes behind and the two small triangles flip upward.

7. Turn the model over.

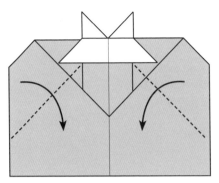

8. Valley fold so the folded edge on top lies on the center (this fold is similar to Step 5 of the Hammerhead).

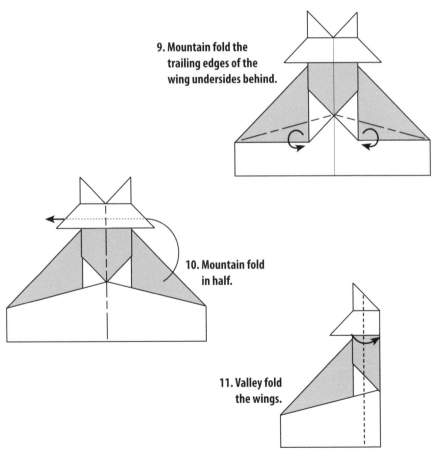

9. Mountain fold the trailing edges of the wing undersides behind.

10. Mountain fold in half.

11. Valley fold the wings.

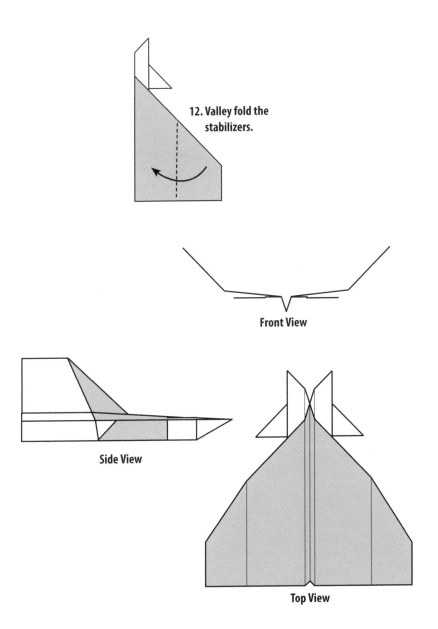

12. Valley fold the stabilizers.

Front View

Side View

Top View

Biplane

Here it is, three years in the making, my biplane.
Use 2 sheets of 8 ½ x 11 inch (A4-size) paper
(that's right, the stuff you've been cutting in half
all along you don't have to cut), and a metallic
portrait of the sixteenth president.

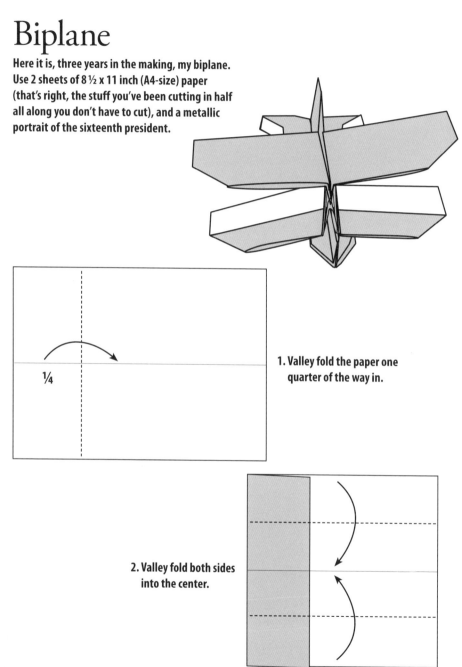

¼

1. Valley fold the paper one
   quarter of the way in.

2. Valley fold both sides
   into the center.

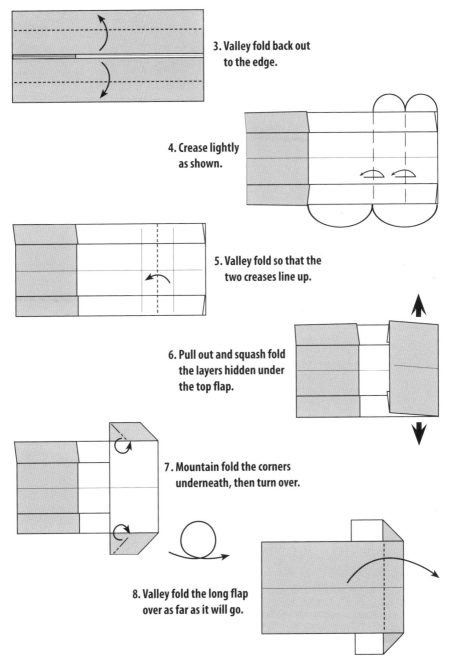

3. Valley fold back out to the edge.

4. Crease lightly as shown.

5. Valley fold so that the two creases line up.

6. Pull out and squash fold the layers hidden under the top flap.

7. Mountain fold the corners underneath, then turn over.

8. Valley fold the long flap over as far as it will go.

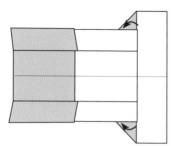

9. Shift the long flap forward as in Step 1 of the Jet Fighter.

10. Flatten the resulting pockets. No landmarks here, just use your best judgment.

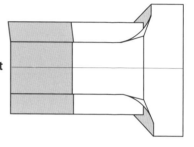

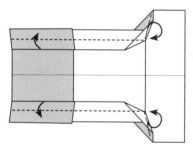

11. Mountain fold the rear of the flap squash folded in the previous step. Valley fold the flaps at the sides in half.

12. Mountain fold the outlying areas behind, then valley fold the model in half.

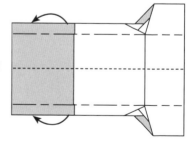

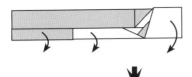

13. Pull down the top layers.

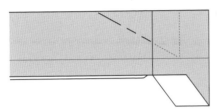

14. Sink the area shown. There's a layer of paper underneath the rightmost section; the sink fold should extend to the lower corner of this layer. Some paper will get pulled out in the process.

15. Sink to form the tail. The sink will continue into the fuselage and should make the tail the same length as the rear wings. Note that a countersink will be needed on the inside of the fuselage.

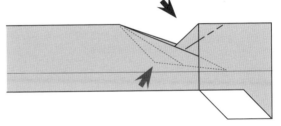

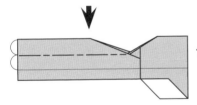

16. Sink once more to narrow the fuselage.

17. Valley fold the rear wings and their supports up perpendicular to the fuselage.

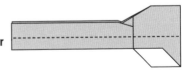

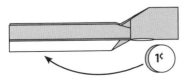

18. Insert a penny into the front. It should be held in place between the layer folded in Step 1 and the rest.

1¢

19. The next series of steps is designed to lock the front end together. Start by reverse folding the bottom flap in on one side only.

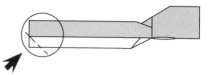

20. Valley fold the inside layer over to lock the top together.

21. View from the top. Crease the side flap along its angle bisector, then crease into fourths.

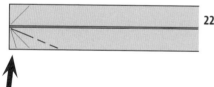

22. Reverse fold along the innermost crease.

23. Part of this is a cutaway view. Roll the reverse folded flap inside along previously made creases. Repeat on the other side.

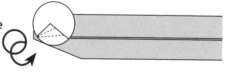

24. Side view again. On the bottom, tuck the flap from one side into the pocket created in Step 20. Round off the top a little with a reverse fold.

Biplane–wings

Another 8½ × 5½ inch (A5-size) sheet of paper creased down the middle is required.

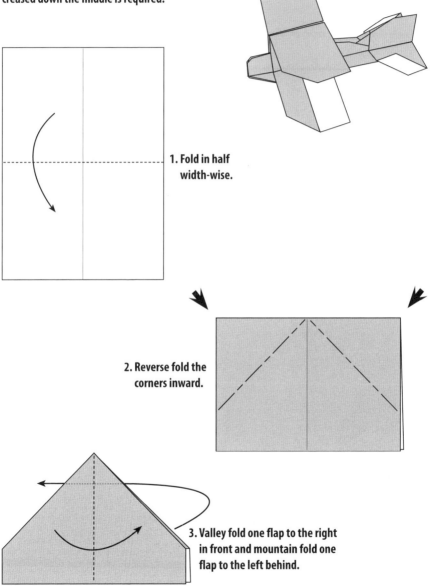

1. Fold in half width-wise.

2. Reverse fold the corners inward.

3. Valley fold one flap to the right in front and mountain fold one flap to the left behind.

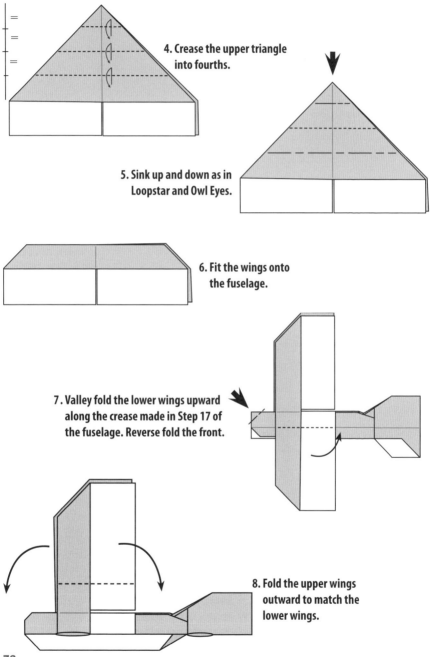

4. Crease the upper triangle into fourths.

5. Sink up and down as in Loopstar and Owl Eyes.

6. Fit the wings onto the fuselage.

7. Valley fold the lower wings upward along the crease made in Step 17 of the fuselage. Reverse fold the front.

8. Fold the upper wings outward to match the lower wings.

9. Sink the paper left over from Step 8 upward.

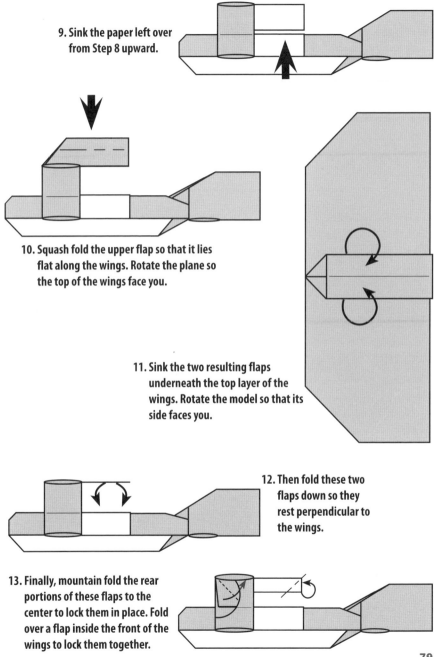

10. Squash fold the upper flap so that it lies flat along the wings. Rotate the plane so the top of the wings face you.

11. Sink the two resulting flaps underneath the top layer of the wings. Rotate the model so that its side faces you.

12. Then fold these two flaps down so they rest perpendicular to the wings.

13. Finally, mountain fold the rear portions of these flaps to the center to lock them in place. Fold over a flap inside the front of the wings to lock them together.

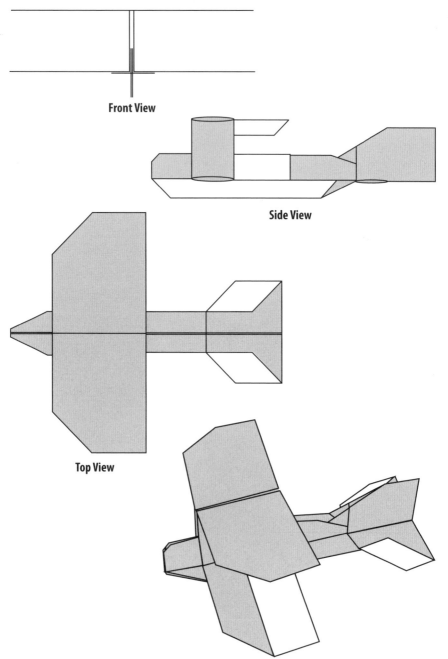

Front View

Side View

Top View